A UNIQUE COLLECTION FOR A UNIQUE MAN

Pictures and stories that capture the essence of a legend

SO many words have been written about Bill Shankly and so many photographs of the Anfield legend published that you may well think there can't possibly be anything left that you haven't read or seen before. You'd be wrong.

In 2012, Trinity Mirror Sport Media published 'Bill Shankly: The Lost Diary' – the story of Liverpool's 1961/62 promotion campaign, in his own words, that had remained in the Liverpool Echo archive for half a century. It captured the imagination of Reds supporters.

Now, to mark the 100th anniversary of the great man's birth in 1913, we bring you 'Shankly 100 – The Unique Collection'.

Not only does this publication feature some of the most iconic, inspiring Shankly images of all time, it also contains some rare and previously unseen photos. It provides a completely new insight into the life and career of one of English football's most famous, inspiring figures. A man who turned Liverpool Football Club from Second Division also-rans into the most successful team in the country.

But this special, commemorative magazine isn't just a magnificent collection of pictures. Chris McLoughlin, the man who pieced together 'Bill Shankly: The Lost Diary', uncovers the stories behind some of them. The tales of Shankly's family life, his managerial genius, the players he worked with and his natural enthusiasm and passion for 'fitba,' as he would call it in his distinctive Scottish accent.

"I was only in the game for the love of football," he once said. "My life is my work. My work is my life." 'Shankly 100 – The Unique Collection' captures Bill's love of life, of work, and of football in all its glory.

And we start with this brilliant photo from 1966...

Design and production by Trinity Mirror Sport Media

Managing Director: Ken Rogers • Senior Editor: Steve Hanrahan • Senior Art Editor: Rick Cooke • Senior Production Editor: Paul Dove
Written by: Chris McLoughlin • Designed by: Alison Barkley & Lee Ashun • Production by: Roy Gilfoyle
Senior Marketing Manager: Claire Brown • Photography: Liverpool Post and Echo archive & Mirrorpix
© Published in Great Britain in 2013 by Trinity Mirror Sport Media, PO Box 48, Old Hall Street, Liverpool, L69 3EB.

ISBN: 9781908695055
Printed by Buxton Press

1

TOP ON POINTS

Perhaps because of what happened in the World Cup that summer, Liverpool's championship success in 1966 is arguably the most unheralded of Shankly's achievements. It was clinched with a 2-1 victory against Chelsea at Anfield on April 30th and as chants of 'ee-aye-adio we've won the league' rang down from the Kop, Shanks held a finger aloft to remind everyone who was top of the pile.

2

SHOOT ON SIGHT

Most top footballers have done glossy magazine photo-shoots at some stage of their careers, but this must have been the first time a Liverpool manager had undertaken such a task. Shanks, at the age of 57, was captured practising his skills down at Melwood in June 1971 and there wasn't an airbrush in sight.

3

DRESSING DOWN

Had Liverpool won at Arsenal on the final day of the 1971/72 season they'd have been crowned champions on goal average, but they drew 0-0 after referee Mr Kirkpatrick wrongly disallowed a John Toshack goal. So angry was Shankly with the decision that he invited the press and photographers into the away dressing room at full-time, even before players such as the pictured Larry Lloyd had got changed, to explain exactly what he thought of the referee. You can probably guess.

4

DOG GONE

Relaxing in the garden of their Bellefield Avenue home in West Derby, Bill, Nessie and grand-daughter Karen play with Scamp, a woolly black poodle that belonged to Karen's Auntie Jean. Shankly adored the dog and would take it for walks down to Everton's Bellefield training ground. He didn't take a poop scoop, either! Sadly, Scamp became ill with a disease that meant all his teeth had to be removed and with the family upset that he could no longer eat solid foods, Shanks said he'd 'take care of it'. Nessie thought he had gone to get a set of doggy dentures fitted for Scamp, but he returned from the vets without the canine. "Where is it, then?" asked Nessie. "I had to put him down," replied Bill. "He's better off. It was the only humane thing to do." The shocked Shankly family put Bill in the dog house for a couple of weeks, but he stuck to his guns. "What's the point of living if you can't ever enjoy a plate of solid food?"

WE'RE THE GREATEST TEAM IN EUROPE AND WE'RE GOING TO ITALY

Shankly and his players were mobbed at the old Liverpool Airport in Speke, now a hotel, as they prepared to fly to Italy for the second leg of the 1965 European Cup semi-final against Inter Milan. The Liverpool manager, his players and the Reds board of directors boarded an Alitalia plane to Italy, but little did they know they were flying into a storm of controversy. Three-one up from the first game at Anfield, Liverpool were beaten 3-0 at an intimidating San Siro – Bob Paisley was struck by a purple smoke bomb – as a result of some hugely questionable refereeing decisions from Jose Maria Ortiz de Mendibil. Shanks later said that the Spanish official would haunt him to his grave.

SIR ROGER RETURNS

Roger Hunt scored 286 goals for Liverpool including a record 245 goals in the league. 278 of those strikes came under the management of Bill Shankly. In 1972, having left the Reds for Bolton in 1969, he returned to Anfield for a testimonial. A crowd of 55,214 packed into Anfield to see Liverpool's 1965 FA Cup winning side reunite and beat an England Select XI 8-6, but not before Shanks had taken the World Cup winner down to see the Kopites who had affectionately dubbed him 'Sir Roger'.

7

GUARD OF HONOUR

Liverpool had all but clinched a record-equalling eighth league title in 1973 by beating Leeds, but confirmed it by taking a point against Leicester City at Anfield. Shankly was given a guard of honour by the Foxes players as he walked onto the pitch to celebrate and later described winning that championship as: "The happiest day of my life. I have known nothing like it as a player or manager. This title gave me greater pleasure than the previous two, simply because here we had a rebuilt side, some of them only two or three seasons in first-team football, and they stayed the course like veterans. I wanted that title more than at any time in my life. That's why it is such a relief."

'The happiest day of **my life**. I have known **nothing like it** as a player or a manager. I wanted **that title** more than at any time in **my life**. That's why it is **such a relief**'

Liverpool skipper Emlyn Hughes gives the boss a hug as they celebrate winning the Division One title in 1973. Having not won the title since 1966 you can see what it meant to Shankly to be holding the Football League trophy again and he celebrated the success both on the pitch with ecstatic young Kopites, with his players and in the dressing room.

9 FLOOD ON FROZEN GROUND

"If you'd seen Anfield when I came it was the biggest toilet in Liverpool. I had to bring water in from Oldfield Road. It cost 3,000 pounds. There was no water to flush the toilets." That was in 1959 and by 1963, ahead of an FA Cup tie against Burnley, the frozen Anfield pitch looked more like a ploughed field than a patch of grass fit for a First Division side. So desperate was Shankly to get the FA Cup fourth round replay on – the original replay had also been called off due to a frozen pitch (top left) – that he called in John Flood, a ground construction expert from Queensferry, to use his tractor-drawn disc harrower to cut through the ice. Bill constantly inspected the pitch himself, but his efforts were to no avail. The game was postponed again and held nine days later with a 119th-minute Ronnie Moran penalty giving the Reds a dramatic late win in front of 57,906 – the biggest Anfield attendance for any cup match during Shankly's time as manager.

10

PITCHING IN

On a snowy December morning in 1964, Shanks arrives at Anfield to join groundsmen and local kids in trying to make the pitch playable ahead of that day's First Division clash with Sunderland. The raking did the trick, but the men from Roker Park held Liverpool to a 0-0 draw.

11

THE BILL SHANKLY BOYS

Two things are unusual about this Liverpool FC team photo from 1971. Firstly, it was taken in the car park at Melwood rather than at Anfield. And secondly, the snap was captured in the January of that year rather than, as per tradition, the previous August. It did, however, mean that John Toshack, who only signed for the club in November 1970, made the photo, but Ian St John, who was sold to South African club Hellenic shortly after scoring against Swansea on January 23, 1971, was missing.

12

RED LEGENDS

Bob Paisley was into the horses more than Shankly, but the Scot didn't need asking twice when the opportunity came to meet the Grand National's greatest horse of all, Red Rum, at Ginger McCain's yard. When Red Rum won Aintree's famous four-mile steeplechase a record three times in 1973, 1974 and 1977, Liverpool won silverware. And when he came second in 1975...so did Liverpool!

13

SHAKE ON IT

It's fair to say youngsters dress rather more casually these days then a teenage Shanks did in this snap!

14

ONBOARD AT ANFIELD

You've almost certainly seen this famous photo of Bill Shankly being welcomed to Anfield as Liverpool manager by chairman Tom Williams in December 1959, but had you ever noticed the pennant on the wall behind them? It bears the logo of HMS Hogue – the Cammell Laird-built battle-class destroyer that was part of the British Pacific Fleet and was used in the film 'Sink the Bismarck'. Quite how the pennant ended up on the wall of TV Williams' office is unknown, but just four months earlier the ship was involved in a collision with the INS Mysore that saw a sailor lose his life and the ship damaged so badly that it had to be broken up.

'Liverpool **came alive** in the 1960s.
The city became **world-famous**
because of the Beatles and **Liverpool
supporters** became world-famous too'

15

OUT ON THE TOWN

After leading Liverpool to their maiden FA Cup success in 1965 and touring the city on an open top bus, Shankly, his players and club directors were invited to a reception at the Liverpool Empire where they were greeted by the Mayor of Liverpool and other local dignitaries.

OFFICIALS & PLAYERS

16

THE HUDDERSFIELD YEARS

April 1959 and on the final weekend of the season, ahead of Huddersfield Town's match at Rotherham United, a photographer was given access to Leeds Road to take pictures of the club's aspirational young manager doing his job. Bill Shankly took the snapper on a tour of the stadium, posing for photos in the dugout, in his office, by his car and at the players' entrance. Eight months later, he was appointed as manager of Liverpool Football Club. "I was leading as peaceful a life as any football manager can lead in the comparatively sheltered calm of Huddersfield," he wrote in the Liverpool ECHO in 1962. "Was I to step out of this into the cauldron-like atmosphere of Anfield to undertake a task which, however much I put into it, could end in failure?" Every Liverpool supporter is thankful that he did.

THE KOP'S MESSIAH

"I'm just one of the people who stands on the Kop. They think the same as I do, and I think the same as they do. It's a kind of marriage of people who like each other."

18

TO SEE SUCH FUN

The night before the 1971 FA Cup final, the Liverpool boss took his players to the London Palladium to chillax, 70s style, by watching 'To See Such Fun'. Honoured to have such illustrious guests in the theatre, comedians Tommy Cooper and Clive Dunn, pianist Russ Conway, plus singer Anita Harris who was sporting a red jersey, invited Bill and his boys onto the stage for a photo. Presumably no-one told Tommy Smith to break a leg – in case he tried to tackle them...

'A football team is like **a piano**. You need eight men to **carry it** and **three** who can **play the damn thing**'

19

A LORRA, LORRA GOALS

And on the training pitch today is our Cilla, all the way from Liverpool. The Scouse singer visited Melwood in 1971 to film an episode of her BBC TV series 'Cilla' although she could possibly have picked better footwear for a kick-about with Shanks and the players! Cilla wasn't the only local celeb to visit Melwood in '71. Ken Dodd turned up to promote his 'Laughing Spectacular' show at the Royal Court. Was Shanks pleased to see him? He was tickled red...

20

HEDGE FUN MANAGER

Golfers are more likely to end up in the rough than football managers, but evidently someone made a mess of a shot during a training session down south ahead of the 1974 FA Cup final. Shanks' attempts to retrieve the lost ball ended with him falling down a ditch, much to the amusement of Steve Heighway, so it was left to skipper Emlyn Hughes to ride to his manager's rescue. The hedge was clearly no match for Liverpool's crazy horse.

21

FIRST CLASS

Proof that the Orient Express wasn't the only train on which you'd find silver service in 1974. After seeing his team thrash Newcastle 3-0 at Wembley, Shankly travelled back to Merseyside with Nessie sat opposite and the FA Cup at his side. We're not sure they needed a train manager to remind passengers to take all their luggage with them that day...

22

FORK-FORK-TWO

Shankly makes some tactical points over the breakfast table aided by cutlery, a bread roll, a bowl of sugar and a cuppa. No wonder Liverpool had their opponents on toast.

23

NEXT STOP WEMBLEY

Shankly smiles for waiting photographers as he gets off the Liverpool team bus ahead of a training session before the 1965 FA Cup final. Reuben Bennett, Shankly's fellow Scot and trusted head coach, leads the players onto the training pitch flanked by a group of local kids armed with over-sized autograph books.

24

MELWOOD MEMORIES

"My first task was to assess the possibilities of the club and by this I mean not only the playing strength but also the staff, equipment and all the facilities. Part of the latter was Melwood which I had not seen prior to accepting my new post. I want to put it on record that my first view of it really staggered me with its potential and elated me when I considered its possibilities." Shankly loved Melwood and this picture from pre-season training in July 1970 shows him laying down his orders.

25

FIGHTING THE SYSTEM

Larry Lloyd and Shankly are all smiles after leaving an FA disciplinary hearing in 1972 having set a new precedent. Strapping centre-half Lloyd and Man City striker Wyn Davies had been dismissed for 'fighting' during Liverpool's 2-0 win over City that August, but it was clear that the only culprit was Davies who had head-butted the Reds' number five. Shankly was so angry with the three-match ban handed to Lloyd by a newly-formed independent disciplinary tribunal that he requested a personal hearing for the player to fight the charge. After reviewing the evidence, the FA quashed Lloyd's ban, thus making Shankly's Liverpool the first side to successfully have such a suspension overturned. It wasn't the only time Shanks appeared at disciplinary hearings with the different expressions on the faces of Ian St John (1963), Chris Lawler and Ian Callaghan (1972) and Tommy Smith (1973) perhaps indicating how well they went!

'The trouble with **referees** is that they **know** the rules, but they don't **know** the game'

26

FULL RANGE OF EMOTIONS

Thoughtful, pensive, tense and even angry, Shanks' face tells the story of the emotions he would go through watching his Liverpool team play. These photos were taken during the Reds' 2-0 win against Manchester United at Old Trafford in April '71 – Stevie Heighway and a Paul Edwards own goal giving Liverpool the victory.

27

STREETS AHEAD

Playing football in the street would probably land you with an ASBO now, but in the 1960s it was encouraged. Shanks watched two teams of Scouse kids having a kick-about on Eldon Grove, off Scotland Road, from one of the flats before going outside to meet them. To be kitted out for street footy tells you how seriously the boys took it.

A PALACE DATE

Bill's wife Nessie joined him outside Buckingham Palace in 1974 as he showed off the OBE he was awarded. "You have been in football a long time," commented The Queen. "Yes, Ma'am," replied Shankly, "it's been 42 years."

29

BILL AND NESSIE

"Ness and I are completely different and she knows absolutely nothing about football. She has never discouraged me from anything I have wanted to do. 'All right, go ahead and do it,' she will say. But she will give her opinion and if I don't accept that opinion, it won't make a difference, not a bit."

30

DEEPDALE DELIGHT

Preston North End's players, including Shankly (third from right), line up for a team photo at Deepdale ahead of the 1938 FA Cup final against Huddersfield Town. Having been on the losing side to Sunderland at Wembley a year earlier, Shanks was determined to get his hands on a winner's medal and did so thanks to a 119th-minute penalty winner from George Mutch.

31

DISC JOCK

Following his retirement in 1974, Shankly took on some media work including holding his own chat show on Radio City. His most notable guest was the pipe-smoking, pint-drinking Prime Minister Harold Wilson. A photo of the pair remains hung on the wall of the staircase of St John's Beacon, Radio City's current home, to this day.

33

BOARDROOM CANTEEN

Having made 19-year-old Alun Evans football's first £100,000 teenager in 1968, Shankly and Liverpool chairman Sid Reakes treated him to tea in the Anfield boardroom. Whatever they fed him did the trick – Evans scored 10 minutes into his debut against Leicester City later that week.

32

SIGN OF THE TIMES

Three different pictures, three different players signed by Bill Shankly. But can you name all three? TV Williams and the rest of the Anfield board joined Shanks when Emlyn Hughes was captured from Blackpool in 1967, while a young Peter Robinson oversaw an even younger Kevin Keegan's transfer from Scunthorpe United in 1971. And the player shaking hands with Bill after completing a move from Crewe Alexandra in 1970? Steve Arnold. While Hughes and Keegan went on to become Kop icons, things didn't work out for Arnold on Merseyside. He made just two first-team appearances for the club before moving on to Rochdale in 1973.

34

A FOND FAREWELL

When footballers leave clubs these days they often do so in the back of a car with a Sky Sports News reporter waving a microphone at the window, but back in the 1960s and 1970s Shankly made a point of publicly saying goodbye to players he was selling. He bid farewell to Tony Hateley in the Anfield boardroom in 1968 – even travelling to Speke Airport to greet the man he was selling him to, Coventry boss Noel Cantwell – and in 1970 posed for a goodbye photo with Geoff Strong.

'For a player to be **good enough** to play for **Liverpool**, he must be prepared to **run through** a brick wall'

35

LISTEN UP, BOYS

Perhaps one of the most famous Shankly images of all, the great man addresses his players in the Anfield dressing room in 1972 ahead of a training session – not that they all appear to be listening!

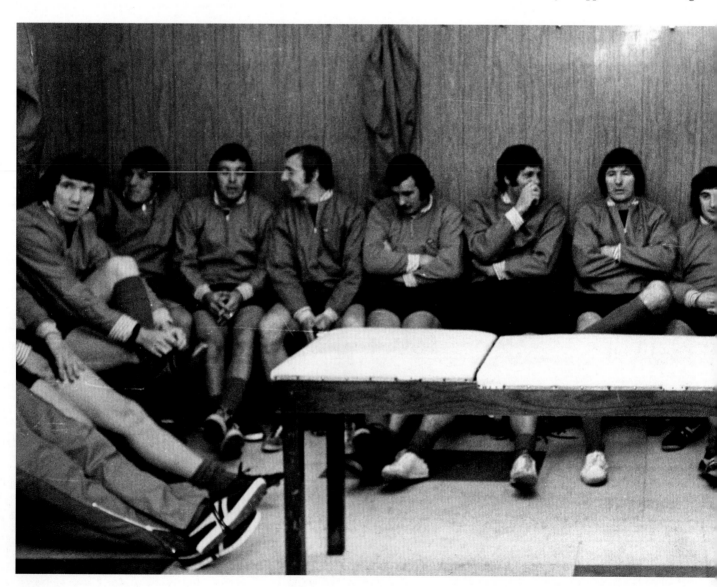

36

NUMBER 10, LIVERPOOL, WILL PLAY...

There was only one way to get the FA Cup draw in the 1960s – listen to the wireless. And that's precisely what Shanks would do ahead of every round. In 1963 he was joined by Bob Paisley, Reuben Bennett and assistant secretary Bill Barlow to hear that Liverpool had been paired with Leicester City in the FA Cup semi-final, while in 1969 he gathered the whole of his squad around the radio to learn their next opponents.

37

FAMILY TIME

Pictured away from the game, for once, Shankly takes time out with his family around the time of his retirement in 1974. He was photographed holding his granddaughter Emma Parry (below), and with Emma and his other granddaughters Pauline Robinson and Karen Gill (right). And in a group family photo (top) there are (back l-r): Nessie, Emma, Pauline, Bill, Karen. (front l-r): Barbara Shankly, Dave Parry, Geoff Carline, Jeanette Shankly.

38

LEADER OF MEN

No Kopite knew it at the time, but a solemn-looking Shankly was leading Liverpool out for an FA Cup final for the last time ahead of the 1974 showpiece against Newcastle. His decision to quit that summer, after leading the club to a second FA Cup success, was a bolt from the red. Despite what was on his mind, he either didn't mention it to Princess Anne before kick-off or she's very good at keeping secrets.

39

WE'LL BE COMING DOWN THE ROAD

Standing on an open top bus with his players – one or two of them wearing some rather garish shirts (mentioning no names, Ray Clemence) – Shankly salutes the thousands upon thousands of Reds who lined the streets to welcome Liverpool's 1974 FA Cup winners back home. The Bill Shankly boys had been slick on the pitch against Newcastle and their bus was sponsored by Schick – a brand of electric shavers that was sold to Phillips in 1981 and is now owned by Energizer Holdings. Maybe they picked the wrong open top bus to sponsor because Liverpool 3 Newcastle 0 was nothing like a close shave for the Redmen.

40

THANKS, SHANKS

There was despair amongst Kopites in 1974 when Shankly announced his shock retirement, but they couldn't let him go without giving him a traditional send-off. So they got him a giant card and handed it around the Kop during his testimonial for everyone to sign! Clearly delighted with it, Bill is pictured at home with his grand-daughters Pauline (left), Emma (centre) and Karen (right). "I'll treasure these presents for the rest of my life," he later said. "They come from people who mean everything to me."

'**I was only** in the game for the **love of football** – and I wanted to bring **happiness** to the people of Liverpool'

41

FITNESS TEST

It's April 1963 and in front of a packed Kop awaiting a rare Monday Merseyside derby, Ian St John takes a fitness test on a well-worn Anfield pitch under the watchful gaze of Bill Shankly and Bob Paisley. It was a test he failed and without the Saint leading the line the Reds were held to a 0-0 draw.

42

A NICE TOUCH

You could get more than a wee dram from this bottle! Shankly celebrates a Bells Scotch Whisky managerial award at Anfield and in 2010 a limited edition Islay-made whisky, Glen of the Buck, was named in Bill's honour after Glenbuck, the village he was from. Only 1892 bottles – a nod to the year of Liverpool FC's formation – were made.

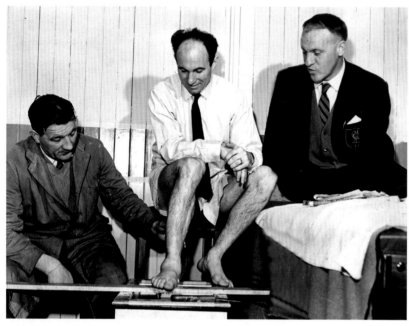

43

WAX ON, WAX OFF

An ever-present throughout the opening 41 games of the 1962/63 campaign, Jimmy Melia's swollen ankle is assessed by Bob Paisley, as a smartly-dressed Shankly looks on, using state-of-the-art medical equipment – a plank of wood placed over a Varitherm paraffin wax bath. Note also the wallpaper scraper that must have been used to scrape the wax off! Unfortunately, there was no miracle cure. Melia was forced to sit out of the '63 FA Cup semi-final against Leicester City at Hillsborough and Liverpool were beaten 1-0.

44

IT'S NOT YOUR KNEE, IT'S LIVERPOOL'S KNEE

Shanks and Bob Paisley inspect the walking wounded – Peter Thompson, Roger Hunt, Ian Callaghan, Gordon Milne and Tommy Smith – during an injury crisis in March 1966.

45

THIS ISN'T ANFIELD

"But that's where I live!" That was Shankly's response to a hotel receptionist in Belgium when he simply wrote 'Anfield' as his home address when checking in ahead of a European game. If the rather stern looking face on the receptionist of the Windsor Hotel – where Liverpool stayed before a 1-1 draw at Fulham in 1964 – is anything to go by then he may well have done the same thing!

46

WEMBLEY '65

Bill Shankly and Don Revie lead out their Liverpool and Leeds United sides at Wembley before meeting the Duke of Edinburgh. If you like a quirky fact or two then how about this? Wembley '65 is the only cup final Liverpool have won using an orange football.

47

RON THE MARCH WITH SHANKLY'S ARMY

'Let's drink six crates to big Ron Yeats, Bill Shankly's pride and joy' sang Kopites and after seeing the Liverpool skipper and his manager celebrate the club's first FA Cup success in 1965, most of them probably did! Even one of the Met's coppers wanted to congratulate Shanks.

48

SEE YOU JIMMY

In one of the most bizarre incidents of the 1970s, an injury to linesman Dennis Drewitt in the September '72 Division One clash between Arsenal and Liverpool at Highbury resulted in former footballer-turned-TV-pundit Jimmy Hill taking over with the flag in a sky-blue tracksuit. A PA announcement had been put out for any qualified referees in the crowd – which Hill was – to step forward so the game could continue. Shankly and Charlie George seemed to find the whole thing rather amusing. The match finished 0-0.

49

THIS IS YOUR LIFE

When Shankly stepped off a Liverpool to London express train in January 1973 en route to the Reds' First Division game at West Ham he was caught by surprise – Eamonn Andrews was waiting for him with a big red book. A seating blunder almost ruined the surprise on platform three at London Euston as the Liverpool party had ended up in the wrong carriage on the train, but realising the error Shankly's team played for time to allow the cameras to get into place. Shankly had spotted the kerfuffle and even

commented "there must be some film stars on board," before stepping off the train to be confronted by Andrews. "As Eamonn Andrews came up to me on the platform I suddenly knew what was going on," he later admitted. "I am overwhelmed by the whole thing and am very proud to have been the subject of the programme." Shanks and his players were whisked away to the This Is Your Life studios the night before the Reds' 1-0 win at Upton Park while Matt Busby and Tommy Docherty were amongst those to pay tribute to him.

50

KEEPING AN EYE ON THE FUTURE

A forward-thinking manager, Shankly created the first Liverpool FC 'nursery' in the summer of 1960, signing up kids such as Tommy Smith, Gordon Wallace and Bobby Graham. By December 1969 he was still planning for the future and is pictured watching a youth team game against Tranmere Rovers at Anfield.

51

STEPPING DOWN

When Shankly announced his retirement on July 12, 1974, it shocked the football world and attracted huge media attention.

'It was like **walking** to the electric chair'

52
HEADS UP!

"It's the greatest thing in the world, natural enthusiasm. You are nothing without it."
As pictures of Shankly go, this snap of him having one of his regular 1950s kick-abouts in a field near Cowrakes, when he was manager of Huddersfield Town, encapsulates his enthusiasm for fitba' perfectly.

53

Sometimes, pictures speak
louder than words. This is
one of them.

54

UNLUCKY HORSESHOE

Shortly before Liverpool took the train down to London for the 1971 FA Cup final against Arsenal, Shankly was handed a lucky horseshoe at Lime Street station. Presumably it came from a horse that had broken a mirror while running underneath a ladder as the Reds went on to lose 2-1 at Wembley.

55

HOMEWARD BOUND

We've all got the train and the bus home, but maybe not quite like this. Shankly, his players and their wives and girlfriends packed out the platform – one or two of them in platforms – at Allerton Station after returning from London following the 1971 cup final. They didn't have a trophy to show off on the open top bus trip through the city centre, but Shanks did wave a red (s)hankie at the thousands who'd come out to have a nose.

56

GOOD CALL

There were no mobiles, smart phones, text messages or Twitter in Shankly's day, just old-fashioned telephones featuring rotary dials. Back in the 1950s and 1960s you had to dial 'ANF' to access numbers in the Anfield district, creating the area code of '263' that remains in use today.

'I want to build a team that's **invincible**, so that they have to **send a team** from Mars to beat us'

57

TROPHY HAUL

Somebody get that man a sideboard!

58

MANAGER OF THE YEAR

Despite his success, Shanks was only named as Bell's Scotch Whisky Football Manager of the Year once in his career after leading Liverpool to a league and UEFA Cup double in 1973. He received the award on a sunny September afternoon before a home game against Chelsea and took it down to the boys on the Spion Kop to give them yet another glimpse of silverware.

59

TELL THEM I TOTALLY DISAGREE WITH WHATEVER THEY ARE SAYING

That famous Shankly quip was made about Italian journalists in 1965, but it is quite apparent from this dressing room photo at Wembley (right) from the same year that he didn't always agree with things that members of the English press said to him! The photographers seemed to get on with Bill much better.

'**Above all**, I would like to be remembered as **a man who was selfless**, who strove and worried so that others could **share the glory**'

SIGNING OUT AT SPURS

Shankly didn't always sit on the Liverpool bench for games. He often opted to sit in the stands to get a different perspective on his team. This picture shows him signing autographs for Tottenham fans at White Hart Lane in May 1974 in what turned out to be an historic match. Nobody, except for Shanks himself, knew it at the time, but the 1-1 draw with Spurs, four days after the FA Cup final, was to be his last official game as Liverpool manager.

61

KEEGAN GETS A WORD IN

Shankly spent so much time addressing the massed ranks of Liverpool fans from the steps of St George's Hall after homecoming parades that he could've had an office there, but at least in 1974 one of his players managed to get hold of the microphone. Thankfully, Kevin Keegan didn't sing!

62

BILL BOY

Liverpool won pretty much everything in the 1960s and 1970s, but there's one thing that the club didn't have. Ball boys. Here Shanks retrieves a couple of stray balls himself during a training session.

63

SNOW BALL

You don't often see a manager having a kick-about with a referee, but Shankly did at a snow-covered Anfield in February 1969 to try and get a game against Nottingham Forest on. Hundreds of volunteers and a Bobcat machine had cleared the pitch the day before only for another overnight snowfall to put the fixture in doubt. However, after 10 minutes of playing with Shanks and Reuben Bennett, the ref, Alan Bone of Sunderland, decided the pitch was playable, although Liverpool had to paint the lines blue! Unfortunately, things didn't work out as planned. Relegation-threatened Forest won 2-0 – the Reds' first Anfield league defeat for 10 months – allowing Leeds to open up a three-point gap at the top of Division One. It proved to be a pivotal weekend in the title race.

64

IT'S THE WAY HE TELLS 'EM

Nessie Shankly and other guests at a July '73 banquet at the Adelphi hotel can't contain their laughter as Bill gives an after-dinner speech.

65

HORSES CLEAR COURSES

You've heard of the White Horse Final of 1923, but perhaps not the white horse of North John Street, 1965. In this previously unpublished picture, a policeman on a white horse tries desperately to clear a path for Liverpool's FA Cup winning team to pass through North John Street on their single-decker open top bus. Can you spot what is missing from the picture, though? Here's a clue. It's silver and would've had red and white ribbons hanging off it...

LIVERPOOL

LIVERPOO F. C

P WINNE

LAWREN

66

NEWCASTLE WERE UNDRESSED

Here are two more great shots from before and after the 1974 FA Cup final victory over Newcastle. After a thoughtful pre-match pitch inspection with Bob Paisley, the man who would soon succeed him as Liverpool manager, Bill congratulates Kevin Keegan and Phil Thompson – wearing the Newcastle number four shirt – after his side's convincing 3-0 win.

67

TAKING COVER

Back in the days when both clubs shared the bench at Wembley, Shankly, Don Revie and members of their backroom teams try to shelter from the rain using tracksuit tops during the 1965 FA Cup final between Liverpool and Leeds. Only a wally would use a brolly at Wembley...

68

HIGH FIVE

Shankly waves to fans waiting at the bottom of the Old Trafford tunnel after leading Liverpool to a 2-1 FA Cup semi-final replay win against Everton in March 1971. Brian Hall was the match-winner, netting his debut goal for the club.

69

FATHER OF THE BRIDE

Bill's daughter Barbara was married to her husband,
Victor Gill, at Brougham Terrace Register Office, West
Derby, on Saturday, January 23, 1965. Naturally, Shanks
was there to give Barbara away, but the ceremony
took place at the somewhat early time of 10am. Why?
Because the Merseyside derby was scheduled for 3pm
that afternoon at Goodison Park and he wasn't planning
on missing it! However, Shankly needn't have worried.
Everton called the game off the day before the wedding
because while their new undersoil heating system had
melted the January snow and frost, it left the pitch
so saturated that it was "a gluepot," as the Liverpool
manager put it. His plan to watch the mini-derby at
Anfield instead that afternoon was also scuppered by the
snow, leaving him spending a Saturday somewhere other
than at a football match for once.

'**Football** follows
you everywhere,
and **eats into**
your family life.
But every working
man **misses out**
on some things
because of **his job**'

70

PROUD DAD

It's not often that the father of the bride is focused upon by a photographer rather than the happy couple, but that's what happened when the Liverpool ECHO turned up to cover the wedding of Shankly's daughter Jeanette to Geoff Carline at Calvary Independent Baptist Church, Knotty Ash, on July 22, 1972. It was a good month for Shanks – he also signed Peter Cormack from Nottingham Forest and the Scottish midfielder turned out to be the final piece of the jigsaw for his second great Liverpool side.

71

HORSE PLAY

Exactly what 'Bless em all' week at Pontins, Blackpool, involved in 1980 is unclear, but Shankly turned up with his hero (and former team-mate) Sir Tom Finney and former Everton player and Man City manager Joe Mercer to take part in a sports quiz. They also found the only horse Bob Paisley hadn't read about in the Racing Post!

72

"Normally managers come into a club and bring their trainers with them. Well I'm not going to do that. You fellows have been here, some of you a long time. I have my own training system and I will work in co-operation with you. I will lay down the plans and gradually we will be on the same wavelength. I want one thing – loyalty. I don't want anybody to carry stories about anyone else. The man with the story will get the sack. I don't care if he has been here for 50 years. I want everyone to be loyal to each other. Everything we do will be for Liverpool Football Club. That makes strength, and maybe one day we'll get the players we need as well." Bob Paisley, Joe Fagan, Ronnie Moran, Reuben Bennett and Tom Saunders gave Bill the loyalty he demanded. And he got those players they needed, too.

73

WHADDYA KNOW, JOE?

Manchester City boss Joe Mercer keeps warm by a Maine Road radiator while chatting with Shankly ahead of Liverpool's game at City in 1971. Bill was also pictured that year chatting with Tottenham boss Bill Nicholson and Burnley's general manager Harry Potts.

74

HANGING OUT WITH FAMILY

Then in charge of Huddersfield, Bill paid a visit back to Scotland in May 1958 to see his brother Bob, manager of Third Lanark FC, hanging out his team's jerseys to dry at Cathkin Park. Who'd heard of a kitman in the 1950s? Third Lanark – the club Liverpool signed player-turned-club secretary Jimmy McInnes from – folded in 1967 and the stadium fell into disrepair, but a pitch and the remains of the terracing are still there to this day and since 2008 it has been the home of a re-formed amateur Third Lanark club.

'At a football club, there's a **holy trinity** – the players, the manager and the **supporters.** Directors are only there to **sign the cheques**'

75

PLATFORM 7 FOR THE NUMBER 10 FROM CARDIFF

Welsh giant John Toshack, with wife Sue, steps off the train at Lime Street Station to be met by his new manager in 1970. Tosh was signed from Cardiff City for £110,000 and despite the platform numbers behind him suggesting which number shirt he might wear, he had number 10 on his back for most of his Anfield career.

76

A SHOW OF RED STRENGTH

"It's questionable if Chairman Mao of China could have arranged such a show of strength as you have shown yesterday and today." Shankly, addressing the crowd on the steps of St George's Hall, after thousands turned up to welcome Liverpool's beaten 1971 FA Cup final side back to the city.

77

TV'S PROGRAMME FOR SUCCESS

Every manager needs a chairman to appoint him in the first place and for Bill Shankly that man was Tom Williams, known to everyone as 'TV'. Shankly's Huddersfield side had beaten Liverpool 5-0 in 1958/59 and after a poor start to the 1959/60 campaign, TV Williams and fellow director Harry Latham approached Shankly in October '59 after travelling to Leeds Road to watch his side face Cardiff City. "Mr Williams said: 'how would you like to manage the best club in the country?' 'Why, is Matt Busby packing up?' I asked." Two months later, an Anfield dynasty had begun.

SIGNING IN, SHAKING HANDS AND SIGNING OUT

Bill welcomes his new £200,000 signing Ray Kennedy to Melwood by telling him he is about to announce his retirement! As inconceivable as it seems, Kennedy was unveiled to press photographers on the same day that Shankly stunned the world of football by quitting Anfield. Outside the ground, some young fans turned up to say their own goodbye to a man every Kopite regarded as irreplaceable.

79

'The **socialism** I believe in is everybody working for **the same goal** and everybody having a **share in the rewards**. That's how I see football, **that's how I see life**'

SHANKLY
100
THE UNIQUE
COLLECTION

80

NOT WORTHY

Summer, 1972, and the maverick Frank Worthington signs in at Anfield under the watchful eyes of Shankly, Bob Paisley and Peter Robinson...only to fail his medical due to high blood pressure. Shanks told him to go away for a break and return for a second examination, but after flying back from Majorca the Huddersfield Town forward failed his medical again because of the same problem and the transfer was shelved. Bill went on to sign Peter Cormack instead while the reasons as to why 23-year-old Worthington had high blood pressure remain the stuff of urban legend!

81

UNDER STARTER'S ORDERS

Stopwatch in hand, Shankly sends (l-r) Dick White, Kevin Lewis, Roger Hunt, Jimmy Melia and Alan A'Court off on a 100m sprint at Melwood. Shouldn't he have held the stopwatch at the finish line?

82

ANOTHER RECORD

In 1971/72 'The Kop Choir' released an LP featuring songs from the famous terrace recorded at games against Chelsea and Bayern Munich. It sold so well that Shankly and Tommy Smith, who appeared on the back of the record sleeve, were presented with a gold disc.

83

SHANKLY AND DIXIE

Shankly and Everton goalscoring legend William Ralph 'Dixie' Dean (right) chat with a 'Mr Howell' in August 1974. Dean died at the Goodison Park Merseyside derby in March 1980 and before the game he and Shankly had stood up and spoken fondly about each other while attending the launch of the Liverpool FC and Everton FC annuals. Shankly is famously quoted as saying at Dean's funeral: "I know this is a sad occasion but I think Dixie would be amazed to know that even in death he could draw a bigger crowd to Goodison than Everton on a Saturday."

84

DOWN ON BENDED KNEE

Remember Dave Brown? The Kopite in a white boiler suit and home-made top-hat who ran onto the Wembley pitch to kiss Shankly's feet after the 1974 Charity Shield? Well these are his predecessors. It was following Liverpool's FA Cup final victory over Newcastle earlier that year when the pair made their way onto the Wembley turf and kissed the great man's shoes in a display of hero-worshipping that encapsulated just how loved the Liverpool manager was.

'I'm a people's man. Only the people matter'

85

PITCH INSPECTION

The day before the 1974 FA Cup final against Newcastle United, Shankly and his staff were invited to inspect the Wembley pitch. If you look closely, you can spot the greyhound traps and track lighting that were still in place around the perimeter of the pitch. Greyhound racing was held at Wembley between 1927 and 1998 and Liverpool came flying out of the traps against the Geordies, beating them 3-0.

86

WE HAD THE BEST TWO TEAMS ON MERSEYSIDE...

Liverpool and Liverpool Reserves. And here's the proof. Shankly attended an end of season dinner for Joe Fagan's Central League winning team of 1969/70. Note the glass full of cigarettes on the table! It was the second consecutive time Liverpool's Reserves had won their league, having not done so since 1958, and they went on a run that saw the club crowned Central League champions every year from 1969 to 1985, with the exceptions of 1972 and 1978. So, when Shanks made his famous 'Liverpool and Liverpool Reserves' quote, he was only half joking.

87

'BOB, I'VE PUT THE WRONG SHORTS ON'

At least that might be why Bill looks a little bit stressed as the annual Liverpool team photo is set up on the Anfield pitch in August 1967. Shankly's side had been playing in all-red for a couple of years by then, but you only have to look at the players standing on the back row to notice there weren't enough sets of red socks to go around for the full squad!

LADBROKE SPORTING CLUB SALUTE

THE HONOURS
SHANKS THE PLAYER
WITH PRESTON
F.A. CUP WINNERS MEDAL 1938
F.A. CUP MEDAL 1937
5 S... INTERNATIONAL CAPS

SH... MANAGER
...POOL
...E DIVISION ONE
1966 1973
...69 1974
...1974

SHANKLYIS...
• THERE ARE TWO G...
  TEAMS IN LIVERPO...
  — LIVERPOOL A...
  LIVERPOOL RESERVES
• RON YEATS IS A
  COLOSSUS. LET ME SHO...
  YOU AROUND HIM
• I DID NOT TAKE MY WIFE...
  CENTRAL LEAGUE MATCH...
  WEDDING ANNIVERSA...
  HER BIRTHDAY
• ...T SO LITTLE SKI...
  ...LDNA TRAP A
  ...CEMENT

88

SHANKLY'S OSCAR

Named as manager of the year in 1973, Shankly is congratulated by Bobby and Jackie Charlton plus Sunderland boss Bob Stokoe. Not even retirement could stop Bill from picking up awards. In 1975 he became the first recipient of the Ladbroke Sporting Oscar, a then-annual award given for outstanding achievement in sport. Shankly was presented with a trophy by his great friend Sir Tom Finney at Ladbroke's Casino in Liverpool with Everton legend Brian Labone, Commonwealth bantam-weight champion Alan Rudkin and ITV commentator Peter Lorenzo amongst those in attendance. Check out the bloke in the foreground about to push the button, presumably so the TV cameras worked!

BOARD MEETING

Pictured at this 1964 Liverpool board meeting, are (l-r): SC Reakes, CJ Hill, H Cartwright, GA Richards, RL Martindale, TV Williams (chairman), JS McInnes (secretary), W Shankly (manager), EAF Sawyer and HK Latham.

FROM NESSIE TO BESSIE

Bessie Braddock, Labour MP for Liverpool Exchange from 1945 to 1970, presents Celtic boss Jock Stein with a manager of the year award at the Cafe Royal in 1966. Shankly also received an award from the fiercely socialist MP, a statue of whom now stands at Lime Street Station, after being named as the 'outstanding manager in league football'.

91

TO CAP IT OFF

After retiring as Liverpool manager in 1974, Shankly returned to Anfield in April '75 for his testimonial against a Don Revie Select XI. He was given a personal thank you on the pitch by Joey Barrett, a well known local character, as he did a lap of honour before kick-off. The attendance was 39,612 – 4,000 more than attended the First Division game with Luton Town that season – and an emotional Shanks addressed the crowd, saying: "I thank the people for their loyalty to me during my years at Liverpool – the greatest part of my whole life. No man can feel more proud, no man can feel more grateful and no man could have more friends than me. This means more to me than anything else. God bless you."

'No man can feel **more proud**, no man can feel **more grateful** and no man could have **more friends** than me'

92

TEA BY THE SEA

Sitting in a Blackpool hotel – possibly the Norbreck Castle in which Shankly holidayed every year – the Liverpool manager takes tea with chairman Tom Williams, director Harry Latham and two of his players, Jimmy Harrower and Bert Slater, in early 1961. Quite what the meeting was about is unknown, but it seems it didn't go well for midfielder Harrower. He was sold to Newcastle United for £15,000 in March of that year.

93

THIS ISN'T WIMBLEDON

Liverpool were so good to watch in 1972/73 that even the Duke of Kent paid a visit to Anfield to take in the Division One clash against Southampton and witnessed five goals, the Reds winning 3-2 thanks to an 87th-minute winner from Kevin Keegan. He was the first royal visitor to Anfield since the 1921 FA Cup semi-final between Wolves and Cardiff City and opened Liverpool's new £600,000 Main Stand. He unveiled a marble plaque without saying a word, but not before Football League president Len Shipman had fallen down a flight of stairs leading up from the foyer and banged his head! The Duke is more used to watching tennis at the All England Club so it must have come as a surprise to see players trying to hit the net rather than miss it. He's pictured in the Main Stand director's box with (l-r) Harold Cartwright, Tom Williams, Eric Sawyer and Bill Shankly who had a direct line down to the dugout to pass on instructions to Bob Paisley and Joe Fagan. FIFA President Sir Stanley Rous was also in attendance.

94

CHAMPIONS!

After clinching the Division One title in 1964, Shankly and his players celebrate with a glass or two of champagne in the Anfield dressing room and on the front row of the Main Stand. The trophy on the table is the 'Curlett Cup' – a home-made cup handed to the players by Kopites to celebrate with because the championship trophy was still at Goodison Park. But not for long!

95

PRE-MATCH BANTER

Having experienced a big Wembley occasion six years earlier, there appears to be no sign of nerves from the great man ahead of the 1971 FA Cup final. The day before the match Shanks shares some banter with Arsenal's Bob Wilson and George Graham before they board their team coach. The Reds boss also caught up with Graham before inspecting the pitch a few hours before kick-off.

96

WEMBLEY INSTRUCTIONS

After an energy-sapping 0-0 draw with Arsenal at a baking hot Wembley, Shanks has a word with Bob Paisley before geeing his troops up for extra-time. His Liverpool side were narrowly beaten in the end, but Shankly still managed a wry smile as the Gunners headed up the Wembley steps to collect their winners' medals.

97

HOLDING COURT

In typically animated fashion, Bill makes a point to journalists he'd invited into his office. Note the pile of letters on the top of the filing cabinet, probably sent to him by Liverpool fans. Shankly would often type out personal replies to his correspondence and in a Liverpool ECHO column in 1962, recently republished as 'Shankly: The Lost Diary', even encouraged supporters to "drop me a line" regarding "these comments or any controversial points."

'A lot of **football success** is in the mind. You must **believe you are the best** and then make sure that **you are**'

FAREWELL

Having surprisingly announced his retirement in the summer of 1974, Shankly said farewell to Liverpool's stunned fans at the Charity Shield at Wembley in what was Brian Clough's first game in his ill-fated 44-day spell in charge of Leeds United. Bill looked pensive on the train down to London and despite having stepped up to replace him and it being his first game as Liverpool boss, Bob Paisley kept a low profile on the day, allowing Shanks to savour the occasion. After a 1-1 draw, the Reds clinched the silverware on penalties – the first penalty shoot-out in Liverpool's history – but the match is perhaps best remembered for the double sending off of Kevin Keegan and Billy Bremner that resulted in both receiving lengthy bans. By the time the pair returned, Clough had been fired.

99

TOUCHLINE TENSION

With a towel draped around his neck, his hands clinched together and Ronnie Moran at his side, a tense looking Shankly watches the second leg of the 1973 UEFA Cup final against Borussia Moenchengladbach in Germany. Three goals up from the first leg at Anfield, the Reds found themselves two goals behind in 39 minutes leaving Shankly, unusually for him, apprehensive and racked with nerves. He spent the final 10 minutes of the game pacing up and down the touchline, shouting at the referee to blow his whistle and chatting with supporters through the wire fence behind him. When the final whistle came it was a blessed relief and Bob Paisley later summed up the tension Shanks had felt: "The second half was the longest 45 minutes of my life."

100

SHANKS

Bill Shankly.
1913-1981.